50 Premium Sandwich Dinner Recipes for Home

By: Kelly Johnson

Table of Contents

- Classic Lobster Roll
- Grilled Cheese with Tomato and Basil
- Beef Brisket Sandwich with BBQ Sauce
- Chicken Parmesan Sandwich
- Italian Meatball Sub
- Smoked Salmon Bagel Sandwich
- Pulled Pork Sandwich with Coleslaw
- Reuben Sandwich with Sauerkraut
- Turkey Avocado Club Sandwich
- Portobello Mushroom Burger
- Chicken Caesar Wrap
- Shrimp Po' Boy with Remoulade
- Caprese Sandwich with Pesto
- Cuban Sandwich with Pickles
- French Dip Sandwich with Au Jus
- Banh Mi with Pickled Vegetables
- Buffalo Chicken Sandwich with Blue Cheese
- Vegan Chickpea Salad Sandwich
- Breakfast Sandwich with Eggs and Bacon
- Tuna Salad Sandwich with Dill
- Philly Cheesesteak Sandwich
- Grilled Veggie and Hummus Wrap
- Jerk Chicken Sandwich with Mango Salsa
- Croque Monsieur with Gruyère Cheese
- Italian Hoagie with Salami and Provolone
- BBQ Chicken Sandwich with Pineapple
- Egg Salad Sandwich with Avocado
- Falafel Pita with Tzatziki Sauce
- Sloppy Joes with Cheddar Cheese
- Gyro Sandwich with Lamb and Tzatziki

- Thai Chicken Sandwich with Peanut Sauce
- Mediterranean Chicken Wrap with Feta
- Spinach and Feta Stuffed Pita
- Pesto Chicken Sandwich with Roasted Red Peppers
- Grilled Ham and Cheese with Apple Slices
- Nashville Hot Chicken Sandwich
- Vegan BBQ Jackfruit Sandwich
- Cilantro Lime Chicken Tacos
- Shrimp Tacos with Avocado Sauce
- Black Bean Burger with Avocado
- Maple Bacon Sandwich with Brie
- Eggplant Parmesan Sandwich
- Chicken Salad Sandwich with Grapes
- Spicy Italian Sausage Sandwich
- Grilled Cheese with Bacon and Avocado
- Roast Beef Sandwich with Horseradish Sauce
- Spinach and Artichoke Dip Sandwich
- Sweet Chili Chicken Sandwich
- Margherita Flatbread Sandwich
- Chicken and Waffle Sandwich

Classic Lobster Roll

Ingredients:

- 1 pound cooked lobster meat, chopped
- 1/4 cup mayonnaise
- 1 tablespoon lemon juice
- 1 tablespoon chopped fresh chives
- 2 tablespoons celery, diced
- Salt and pepper to taste
- 4 hot dog buns
- Butter for toasting

Instructions:

1. In a bowl, combine lobster meat, mayonnaise, lemon juice, chives, celery, salt, and pepper. Mix gently to combine.
2. Heat butter in a skillet over medium heat. Toast the hot dog buns until golden brown.
3. Fill each bun with the lobster mixture and serve immediately.

Grilled Cheese with Tomato and Basil

Ingredients:

- 4 slices of bread
- 2 tablespoons butter
- 4 slices of cheddar cheese
- 1 large tomato, sliced
- Fresh basil leaves
- Salt and pepper to taste

Instructions:

1. Heat a skillet over medium heat. Butter one side of each slice of bread.
2. Place two slices in the skillet, buttered side down. Layer with cheddar cheese, tomato slices, basil leaves, salt, and pepper.
3. Top with the remaining bread slices, buttered side up. Cook until golden brown, about 3-4 minutes per side, until the cheese is melted.
4. Slice in half and serve warm.

Beef Brisket Sandwich with BBQ Sauce

Ingredients:

- 1 pound beef brisket, cooked and sliced
- 1 cup BBQ sauce
- 4 sandwich buns
- Pickles and coleslaw for serving

Instructions:

1. Heat the sliced brisket in a saucepan over medium heat, adding BBQ sauce until heated through.
2. Toast the sandwich buns lightly.
3. Assemble the sandwiches by placing BBQ brisket on the bottom half of each bun, topping with pickles and coleslaw.
4. Place the top half of the bun on and serve warm.

Chicken Parmesan Sandwich

Ingredients:

- 1 pound chicken breasts, flattened
- 1 cup breadcrumbs
- 1/2 cup grated Parmesan cheese
- 1 cup marinara sauce
- 4 slices of mozzarella cheese
- 4 sandwich rolls
- Olive oil for frying

Instructions:

1. Preheat the oven to 375°F (190°C).
2. In a bowl, combine breadcrumbs and Parmesan cheese. Dip chicken breasts in the breadcrumb mixture, then fry in olive oil until golden brown.
3. Place the fried chicken on a baking sheet, top with marinara sauce and mozzarella cheese. Bake for 10-15 minutes until the cheese is melted.
4. Serve on sandwich rolls.

Italian Meatball Sub

Ingredients:

- 1 pound ground beef
- 1/2 cup breadcrumbs
- 1/4 cup grated Parmesan cheese
- 1 egg
- 1 cup marinara sauce
- 4 sub rolls
- Fresh basil for garnish

Instructions:

1. Preheat the oven to 375°F (190°C). In a bowl, combine ground beef, breadcrumbs, Parmesan cheese, and egg. Form into meatballs.
2. Bake meatballs for 20-25 minutes until cooked through.
3. In a saucepan, heat marinara sauce and add the cooked meatballs.
4. Serve meatballs on sub rolls, garnished with fresh basil.

Smoked Salmon Bagel Sandwich

Ingredients:

- 4 bagels, split
- 8 oz cream cheese
- 8 oz smoked salmon
- 1 small red onion, thinly sliced
- Capers for garnish
- Fresh dill for garnish

Instructions:

1. Spread cream cheese generously on each half of the bagels.
2. Layer smoked salmon, red onion slices, and capers on the bottom half of each bagel.
3. Top with the other half of the bagel and garnish with fresh dill before serving.

Pulled Pork Sandwich with Coleslaw

Ingredients:

- 1 pound pulled pork, cooked
- 1 cup BBQ sauce
- 4 sandwich buns
- 1 cup coleslaw mix
- 1/4 cup coleslaw dressing

Instructions:

1. In a saucepan, heat pulled pork with BBQ sauce over medium heat until warm.
2. In a bowl, combine coleslaw mix and dressing.
3. Toast the sandwich buns lightly.
4. Assemble the sandwiches by placing pulled pork on the bottom half of each bun and topping with coleslaw.
5. Place the top half of the bun on and serve warm.

Reuben Sandwich with Sauerkraut

Ingredients:

- 8 slices rye bread
- 1 pound corned beef, sliced
- 1 cup sauerkraut, drained
- 8 slices Swiss cheese
- 1/4 cup Thousand Island dressing
- Butter for grilling

Instructions:

1. Preheat a skillet over medium heat.
2. Spread butter on one side of each slice of rye bread.
3. On the unbuttered side, layer corned beef, sauerkraut, Swiss cheese, and Thousand Island dressing.
4. Top with another slice of bread, buttered side up.
5. Grill until golden brown on both sides and the cheese is melted, about 3-4 minutes per side.
6. Slice in half and serve hot.

Turkey Avocado Club Sandwich

Ingredients:

- 8 slices whole grain bread
- 1 pound sliced turkey breast
- 1 avocado, sliced
- 4 slices bacon, cooked
- Lettuce leaves
- Tomato slices
- Mayonnaise

Instructions:

1. Toast the bread slices until golden.
2. Spread mayonnaise on one side of each slice.
3. Layer turkey, avocado, bacon, lettuce, and tomato on four slices of bread.
4. Top with the remaining slices to form sandwiches.
5. Cut into quarters and serve.

Portobello Mushroom Burger

Ingredients:

- 4 large portobello mushrooms, stems removed
- 1/4 cup balsamic vinegar
- 2 tablespoons olive oil
- 4 hamburger buns
- Lettuce, tomato, and onion for toppings
- Cheese slices (optional)

Instructions:

1. Preheat grill or skillet over medium-high heat.
2. Marinate mushrooms in balsamic vinegar and olive oil for 15 minutes.
3. Grill mushrooms for about 5 minutes on each side until tender.
4. Toast the hamburger buns.
5. Assemble the burgers with grilled mushrooms, cheese (if using), lettuce, tomato, and onion.

Chicken Caesar Wrap

Ingredients:

- 2 cups cooked chicken, diced
- 1 cup romaine lettuce, chopped
- 1/2 cup Caesar dressing
- 1/4 cup grated Parmesan cheese
- 4 large flour tortillas

Instructions:

1. In a bowl, mix together chicken, lettuce, Caesar dressing, and Parmesan cheese.
2. Place a generous amount of the mixture onto each tortilla.
3. Roll the tortillas tightly to form wraps.
4. Cut in half and serve.

Shrimp Po' Boy with Remoulade

Ingredients:

- 1 pound shrimp, peeled and deveined
- 1 cup buttermilk
- 1 cup cornmeal
- 1/2 cup all-purpose flour
- Oil for frying
- 4 hoagie rolls
- Lettuce and tomato for toppings
- 1/2 cup remoulade sauce

Instructions:

1. Soak shrimp in buttermilk for 30 minutes.
2. In a bowl, mix cornmeal and flour.
3. Heat oil in a deep skillet. Dredge shrimp in the cornmeal mixture and fry until golden brown, about 3-4 minutes.
4. Toast hoagie rolls.
5. Assemble the sandwiches with fried shrimp, lettuce, tomato, and remoulade sauce.

Caprese Sandwich with Pesto

Ingredients:

- 4 ciabatta rolls
- 8 oz fresh mozzarella cheese, sliced
- 2 large tomatoes, sliced
- Fresh basil leaves
- 1/4 cup pesto sauce
- Balsamic glaze for drizzling

Instructions:

1. Preheat the oven to 375°F (190°C).
2. Cut ciabatta rolls in half and spread pesto on the cut sides.
3. Layer mozzarella, tomato slices, and basil on the bottom half of each roll.
4. Drizzle with balsamic glaze and place the top half of the roll on.
5. Bake for 10-15 minutes until the cheese is melted and the bread is toasted.

Cuban Sandwich with Pickles

Ingredients:

- 4 Cuban bread rolls
- 1 pound sliced pork, cooked
- 1/2 pound sliced ham
- 1/2 pound Swiss cheese
- 1/4 cup mustard
- 1/2 cup dill pickles, sliced

Instructions:

1. Preheat a panini press or skillet.
2. Spread mustard on the inside of each Cuban roll.
3. Layer pork, ham, Swiss cheese, and pickles on the bottom half of each roll.
4. Place the top half of the roll on and press in the panini press or skillet until the bread is toasted and the cheese is melted, about 5-7 minutes.
5. Slice in half and serve warm.

French Dip Sandwich with Au Jus

Ingredients:

- 4 hoagie rolls
- 1 pound roast beef, sliced
- 1 cup beef broth
- 1 cup provolone cheese, sliced
- 1 onion, thinly sliced
- 2 tablespoons olive oil
- Salt and pepper to taste

Instructions:

1. Preheat the oven to 350°F (175°C).
2. In a skillet, heat olive oil over medium heat. Sauté onions until caramelized, about 10 minutes.
3. Place sliced roast beef in the beef broth in a pot and warm over low heat.
4. Split the hoagie rolls and layer with roast beef, caramelized onions, and provolone cheese.
5. Bake for 5-7 minutes until the cheese melts. Serve with warm au jus for dipping.

Banh Mi with Pickled Vegetables

Ingredients:

- 4 baguette rolls
- 1 pound cooked pork or chicken, sliced
- 1 cucumber, sliced
- 1 carrot, julienned
- 1 daikon radish, julienned
- 1/2 cup mayonnaise
- 1/4 cup pickled vegetables
- Fresh cilantro leaves
- Jalapeños, sliced (optional)

Instructions:

1. Pickle carrots and daikon radish in vinegar for at least 30 minutes.
2. Spread mayonnaise on the baguette rolls.
3. Layer with meat, cucumber, pickled vegetables, cilantro, and jalapeños.
4. Close the baguette and serve fresh.

Buffalo Chicken Sandwich with Blue Cheese

Ingredients:

- 1 pound cooked chicken, shredded
- 1/2 cup buffalo sauce
- 4 hamburger buns
- 1/2 cup blue cheese crumbles
- Lettuce for topping
- Ranch or blue cheese dressing

Instructions:

1. In a bowl, mix shredded chicken with buffalo sauce.
2. Toast hamburger buns.
3. Place buffalo chicken on each bun, top with lettuce and blue cheese crumbles.
4. Drizzle with ranch or blue cheese dressing before serving.

Vegan Chickpea Salad Sandwich

Ingredients:

- 1 can chickpeas, drained and rinsed
- 1/4 cup vegan mayo
- 1 tablespoon Dijon mustard
- 1 celery stalk, chopped
- 1/4 cup red onion, diced
- Salt and pepper to taste
- 4 slices whole grain bread
- Lettuce for serving

Instructions:

1. In a bowl, mash chickpeas with a fork.
2. Stir in vegan mayo, Dijon mustard, celery, onion, salt, and pepper.
3. Spread the chickpea mixture onto bread slices and top with lettuce.
4. Assemble the sandwich and serve.

Breakfast Sandwich with Eggs and Bacon

Ingredients:

- 4 English muffins
- 8 slices bacon
- 4 eggs
- 4 slices cheddar cheese
- Butter for toasting

Instructions:

1. Cook bacon in a skillet until crispy.
2. In the same skillet, fry eggs to your desired doneness.
3. Split and toast the English muffins.
4. Assemble the sandwiches by layering bacon, egg, and cheese on each muffin half.
5. Close the sandwich and serve warm.

Tuna Salad Sandwich with Dill

Ingredients:

- 1 can tuna, drained
- 1/4 cup mayonnaise
- 1 tablespoon Dijon mustard
- 1 tablespoon dill pickle relish
- 1 tablespoon fresh dill, chopped
- Salt and pepper to taste
- 4 slices whole grain bread
- Lettuce for serving

Instructions:

1. In a bowl, combine tuna, mayonnaise, mustard, relish, dill, salt, and pepper.
2. Mix until well combined.
3. Spread the tuna salad onto slices of bread and top with lettuce.
4. Close the sandwiches and serve.

Philly Cheesesteak Sandwich

Ingredients:

- 1 pound ribeye steak, thinly sliced
- 1 onion, sliced
- 1 green bell pepper, sliced
- 4 hoagie rolls
- 1 cup provolone cheese, sliced
- Olive oil for cooking
- Salt and pepper to taste

Instructions:

1. Heat olive oil in a skillet over medium heat. Sauté onions and peppers until softened.
2. Add the sliced steak, seasoning with salt and pepper, and cook until browned.
3. Split the hoagie rolls and fill with the steak mixture.
4. Top with provolone cheese and place under the broiler until the cheese is melted.
5. Serve hot.

Grilled Veggie and Hummus Wrap

Ingredients:

- 4 large tortillas or wraps
- 1 zucchini, sliced
- 1 bell pepper, sliced
- 1 red onion, sliced
- 1 cup hummus
- Olive oil for grilling
- Salt and pepper to taste
- Fresh spinach or arugula

Instructions:

1. Preheat the grill or grill pan over medium heat.
2. Toss the zucchini, bell pepper, and onion with olive oil, salt, and pepper. Grill until tender and slightly charred, about 5-7 minutes.
3. Spread hummus on each tortilla.
4. Layer with grilled veggies and fresh spinach or arugula.
5. Roll tightly, slice in half, and serve.

Jerk Chicken Sandwich with Mango Salsa

Ingredients:

- 4 chicken breasts
- 2 tablespoons jerk seasoning
- 4 hamburger buns
- 1 mango, diced
- 1/2 red onion, diced
- 1 lime, juiced
- Lettuce for serving

Instructions:

1. Rub chicken breasts with jerk seasoning and grill until fully cooked.
2. In a bowl, combine diced mango, red onion, lime juice, salt, and pepper to make the salsa.
3. Toast the hamburger buns.
4. Assemble the sandwich with grilled chicken, mango salsa, and lettuce.
5. Serve with additional salsa on the side.

Croque Monsieur with Gruyère Cheese

Ingredients:

- 8 slices bread
- 4 slices ham
- 4 slices Gruyère cheese
- 1/4 cup butter
- 1/4 cup all-purpose flour
- 1 cup milk
- 1 tablespoon Dijon mustard
- Salt and pepper to taste

Instructions:

1. Preheat the oven to 400°F (200°C).
2. In a saucepan, melt butter, stir in flour, and cook for 1 minute. Gradually whisk in milk and cook until thickened. Season with mustard, salt, and pepper.
3. Assemble sandwiches with ham and Gruyère between two slices of bread.
4. Spread the white sauce on top and bake for 10-15 minutes until golden and bubbly.
5. Serve hot.

Italian Hoagie with Salami and Provolone

Ingredients:

- 4 hoagie rolls
- 1/2 pound salami, sliced
- 1/2 pound provolone cheese, sliced
- Lettuce, shredded
- Tomato, sliced
- Olive oil and red wine vinegar for drizzling
- Salt and pepper to taste

Instructions:

1. Split the hoagie rolls and layer with salami and provolone cheese.
2. Add shredded lettuce and tomato slices.
3. Drizzle with olive oil, red wine vinegar, salt, and pepper.
4. Close the sandwich, slice, and serve.

BBQ Chicken Sandwich with Pineapple

Ingredients:

- 4 cooked chicken breasts, shredded
- 1 cup BBQ sauce
- 4 hamburger buns
- 1 cup pineapple rings, grilled
- Coleslaw for topping

Instructions:

1. In a bowl, mix shredded chicken with BBQ sauce until well coated.
2. Heat the BBQ chicken mixture in a skillet until warm.
3. Toast the hamburger buns.
4. Assemble the sandwiches with BBQ chicken, grilled pineapple, and coleslaw on top.
5. Serve immediately.

Egg Salad Sandwich with Avocado

Ingredients:

- 6 hard-boiled eggs, chopped
- 1/4 cup mayonnaise
- 1 tablespoon Dijon mustard
- 1 avocado, mashed
- Salt and pepper to taste
- 4 slices whole grain bread
- Lettuce for serving

Instructions:

1. In a bowl, combine chopped eggs, mayonnaise, mustard, mashed avocado, salt, and pepper.
2. Mix until well combined.
3. Spread the egg salad mixture onto slices of bread and top with lettuce.
4. Close the sandwiches and serve.

Falafel Pita with Tzatziki Sauce

Ingredients:

- 1 package falafel mix or homemade falafel
- 4 pita breads
- 1 cup tzatziki sauce
- 1 cucumber, sliced
- Lettuce or mixed greens

Instructions:

1. Prepare falafel according to package instructions or recipe.
2. Warm pita breads in a skillet or oven.
3. Fill each pita with falafel, sliced cucumber, and greens.
4. Drizzle with tzatziki sauce and serve.

Sloppy Joes with Cheddar Cheese

Ingredients:

- 1 pound ground beef
- 1 small onion, chopped
- 1 cup ketchup
- 2 tablespoons Worcestershire sauce
- 1 tablespoon brown sugar
- 1 tablespoon mustard
- Salt and pepper to taste
- 4 hamburger buns
- 1 cup shredded cheddar cheese

Instructions:

1. In a skillet, brown the ground beef with chopped onion over medium heat. Drain excess fat.
2. Stir in ketchup, Worcestershire sauce, brown sugar, mustard, salt, and pepper. Simmer for about 10 minutes.
3. Toast hamburger buns, then spoon the beef mixture onto the bottom halves.
4. Top with shredded cheddar cheese, then cover with the top halves. Serve hot.

Gyro Sandwich with Lamb and Tzatziki

Ingredients:

- 1 pound ground lamb
- 1 teaspoon garlic powder
- 1 teaspoon onion powder
- 1 teaspoon dried oregano
- Salt and pepper to taste
- Pita bread
- 1 cup tzatziki sauce
- Lettuce, tomato, and onion for toppings

Instructions:

1. In a bowl, mix ground lamb with garlic powder, onion powder, oregano, salt, and pepper. Form into patties.
2. Cook patties on a grill or skillet until fully cooked.
3. Warm pita bread, then place the cooked lamb inside.
4. Top with tzatziki sauce, lettuce, tomato, and onion. Fold and serve.

Thai Chicken Sandwich with Peanut Sauce

Ingredients:

- 2 cooked chicken breasts, shredded
- 1/4 cup peanut sauce
- 4 sandwich rolls
- Sliced cucumber and carrots for topping
- Fresh cilantro for garnish

Instructions:

1. In a bowl, mix shredded chicken with peanut sauce until well coated.
2. Toast sandwich rolls, then fill with the peanut chicken mixture.
3. Top with sliced cucumber, carrots, and fresh cilantro. Serve immediately.

Mediterranean Chicken Wrap with Feta

Ingredients:

- 2 cooked chicken breasts, sliced
- 4 large tortillas or wraps
- 1/2 cup feta cheese, crumbled
- 1 cup mixed greens
- 1/2 cup cherry tomatoes, halved
- Olive oil and lemon juice for dressing

Instructions:

1. In a bowl, toss chicken slices, mixed greens, cherry tomatoes, feta cheese, olive oil, and lemon juice.
2. Place the mixture in the center of each tortilla and wrap tightly.
3. Slice in half and serve.

Spinach and Feta Stuffed Pita

Ingredients:

- 1 cup fresh spinach, chopped
- 1/2 cup feta cheese, crumbled
- 1/4 cup cream cheese, softened
- Salt and pepper to taste
- Pita bread

Instructions:

1. In a bowl, mix chopped spinach, feta cheese, cream cheese, salt, and pepper.
2. Cut the pita bread in half to form pockets.
3. Stuff each pocket with the spinach and feta mixture. Serve chilled or at room temperature.

Pesto Chicken Sandwich with Roasted Red Peppers

Ingredients:

- 2 cooked chicken breasts, sliced
- 1/4 cup pesto sauce
- 4 ciabatta rolls
- 1/2 cup roasted red peppers, sliced
- Fresh arugula or spinach

Instructions:

1. In a bowl, toss sliced chicken with pesto sauce until well coated.
2. Toast ciabatta rolls, then layer with pesto chicken, roasted red peppers, and arugula.
3. Close the sandwiches and serve.

Grilled Ham and Cheese with Apple Slices

Ingredients:

- 8 slices bread
- 4 slices ham
- 4 slices cheese (cheddar or Swiss)
- 4 tablespoons butter
- 1 apple, thinly sliced

Instructions:

1. Heat a skillet over medium heat.
2. Butter one side of each slice of bread.
3. Layer ham, cheese, and apple slices between two slices of bread (buttered side out).
4. Grill until golden brown on both sides and cheese is melted, about 3-4 minutes per side. Serve warm.

Nashville Hot Chicken Sandwich

Ingredients:

- 2 chicken breasts
- 1 cup buttermilk
- 1 cup flour
- 1 tablespoon cayenne pepper
- 1 teaspoon paprika
- 1 teaspoon garlic powder
- 1 teaspoon salt
- 1/2 cup vegetable oil
- 4 sandwich buns
- Pickles for garnish

Instructions:

1. Soak the chicken breasts in buttermilk for at least 1 hour.
2. In a bowl, mix flour, cayenne pepper, paprika, garlic powder, and salt.
3. Coat the chicken in the flour mixture.
4. Heat oil in a skillet and fry the chicken until golden and cooked through.
5. Toast sandwich buns, place the fried chicken on the buns, and garnish with pickles. Serve hot.

Vegan BBQ Jackfruit Sandwich

Ingredients:

- 1 can young jackfruit, drained and shredded
- 1 cup BBQ sauce
- 4 sandwich rolls
- Coleslaw for topping

Instructions:

1. Heat the jackfruit in a skillet over medium heat until softened.
2. Stir in BBQ sauce and cook until heated through.
3. Toast sandwich rolls and fill with BBQ jackfruit.
4. Top with coleslaw and serve.

Cilantro Lime Chicken Tacos

Ingredients:

- 2 cooked chicken breasts, shredded
- 1/4 cup lime juice
- 1/4 cup chopped cilantro
- 8 small tortillas
- Sliced avocado for topping

Instructions:

1. In a bowl, mix shredded chicken with lime juice and cilantro.
2. Warm tortillas and fill with chicken mixture.
3. Top with sliced avocado and serve.

Shrimp Tacos with Avocado Sauce

Ingredients:

- 1 pound shrimp, peeled and deveined
- 1 tablespoon olive oil
- 1 teaspoon chili powder
- 8 small tortillas
- 1 avocado
- 1/4 cup sour cream
- Juice of 1 lime

Instructions:

1. Season shrimp with chili powder and cook in olive oil until done.
2. In a blender, mix avocado, sour cream, and lime juice to make the sauce.
3. Fill tortillas with shrimp and drizzle with avocado sauce. Serve.

Black Bean Burger with Avocado

Ingredients:

- 1 can black beans, drained
- 1/4 cup breadcrumbs
- 1 teaspoon cumin
- 1 avocado, sliced
- 4 burger buns

Instructions:

1. Mash black beans in a bowl and mix with breadcrumbs and cumin. Form into patties.
2. Cook patties in a skillet until browned.
3. Toast burger buns and fill with black bean patties and avocado slices. Serve.

Maple Bacon Sandwich with Brie

Ingredients:

- 8 slices bacon
- 4 sandwich rolls
- 4 slices Brie cheese
- 2 tablespoons maple syrup

Instructions:

1. Cook bacon until crispy.
2. Toast sandwich rolls and layer with Brie, bacon, and a drizzle of maple syrup.
3. Serve warm.

Eggplant Parmesan Sandwich

Ingredients:

- 1 large eggplant, sliced
- 1 cup marinara sauce
- 4 sandwich rolls
- 1/2 cup grated Parmesan cheese
- 1/2 cup mozzarella cheese

Instructions:

1. Bread and fry eggplant slices until golden.
2. Toast sandwich rolls and layer with marinara sauce, fried eggplant, and cheeses.
3. Broil briefly to melt the cheese, then serve.

Chicken Salad Sandwich with Grapes

Ingredients:

- 2 cooked chicken breasts, diced
- 1/2 cup mayonnaise
- 1/4 cup sliced grapes
- 4 sandwich rolls
- Lettuce for garnish

Instructions:

1. In a bowl, mix diced chicken, mayonnaise, and grapes.
2. Toast sandwich rolls and fill with chicken salad.
3. Garnish with lettuce and serve.

Please enjoy these recipes!

Spicy Italian Sausage Sandwich

Ingredients:

- 4 spicy Italian sausages
- 4 sandwich rolls
- 1 cup marinara sauce
- 1/2 cup sliced bell peppers
- 1/2 cup sliced onions
- Grated Parmesan cheese for topping

Instructions:

1. Grill or pan-fry the sausages until cooked through.
2. Sauté the bell peppers and onions until tender.
3. Warm the marinara sauce.
4. Toast the sandwich rolls and fill with sausages, sautéed vegetables, and marinara sauce.
5. Top with grated Parmesan cheese and serve.

Grilled Cheese with Bacon and Avocado

Ingredients:

- 8 slices of bread
- 4 slices of cheese (cheddar or your choice)
- 4 slices of cooked bacon
- 1 avocado, sliced
- Butter for grilling

Instructions:

1. Butter one side of each slice of bread.
2. Layer cheese, bacon, and avocado between two slices of bread, buttered side out.
3. Grill in a skillet over medium heat until golden brown and cheese is melted.
4. Cut in half and serve.

Roast Beef Sandwich with Horseradish Sauce

Ingredients:

- 8 oz thinly sliced roast beef
- 4 sandwich rolls
- 1/4 cup horseradish sauce
- Lettuce and tomato slices for topping

Instructions:

1. Spread horseradish sauce on the inside of each sandwich roll.
2. Layer roast beef, lettuce, and tomato on the rolls.
3. Close the sandwiches and serve.

Spinach and Artichoke Dip Sandwich

Ingredients:

- 1 cup spinach and artichoke dip (store-bought or homemade)
- 4 sandwich rolls
- 1/2 cup shredded mozzarella cheese

Instructions:

1. Preheat the oven to 350°F (175°C).
2. Fill each sandwich roll with spinach and artichoke dip and top with mozzarella cheese.
3. Place on a baking sheet and bake until the cheese is melted and bubbly.
4. Serve warm.

Sweet Chili Chicken Sandwich

Ingredients:

- 2 cooked chicken breasts, shredded
- 1/4 cup sweet chili sauce
- 4 sandwich rolls
- Lettuce and cucumber slices for topping

Instructions:

1. Mix shredded chicken with sweet chili sauce.
2. Toast the sandwich rolls and fill with the chicken mixture.
3. Top with lettuce and cucumber slices, then serve.

Margherita Flatbread Sandwich

Ingredients:

- 2 flatbreads
- 1 cup fresh mozzarella cheese, sliced
- 1 tomato, sliced
- Fresh basil leaves
- Balsamic glaze for drizzling

Instructions:

1. Preheat the oven to 400°F (200°C).
2. Layer mozzarella and tomato slices on flatbreads.
3. Bake for about 10 minutes, or until the cheese is melted.
4. Top with fresh basil and drizzle with balsamic glaze before serving.

Chicken and Waffle Sandwich

Ingredients:

- 2 waffles
- 1 cooked chicken breast, fried or grilled
- Maple syrup for drizzling
- Butter for waffles

Instructions:

1. Toast or warm the waffles.
2. Place the cooked chicken breast between two waffles.
3. Drizzle with maple syrup and serve warm.

Enjoy these delicious sandwich recipes!

www.ingramcontent.com/pod-product-compliance
Lightning Source LLC
LaVergne TN
LVHW081501060526
838201LV00056BA/2865